Remnants and Yarns

Poverty and protest
in the woollen industry
in Bradford on Avon

Produced by Watermarx
Published by White Horse (Wiltshire) Trades Council.

Published in 2022
by
White Horse (Wiltshire) Trades Council

Produced by
WaterMarx
www.watermarx.co.uk

ISBN 978-0-9957917-1-8

Printed by Sarum Colourview
Unit 8, Woodford Centre
Lysander Way, Old Sarum, Salisbury SP4 6BU
01722 343600
www.sarumcolourview.co.uk

Disclaimer
Views expressed in this publication are those of the author
and not necessarily those of WaterMarx or White Horse
(Wiltshire) Trades Council

Contents

Cover picture: Bradford on Avon Town Bridge by Bob Naylor/Watermarx Media©

Dedication

I would like to dedicate Remnants and Yarns to my former history teacher Mr Curry at Ernest Bailey Grammar School in Matlock.

He made history accessible with an unerring energy and enthusiasm, which inspired in me a life-long love of history and the historic environment.

His teaching of the A level syllabus which included British political history 1815 to 1914 was so vivid and memorable that even after half a century it has served me well in the background to compiling this account.

Rosie MacGregor grew up in Derbyshire, attended university in Bristol and has lived in Bradford on Avon since 1979.

She is also well known as folk singer and music journalist Rosie Upton.

Rosie is a trade union activist and in a career in architecture and town planning has specialised in the historic built environment.

Introduction

I grew up in Matlock in Derbyshire on the hillside above Lumsdale, an historic mill site where I played in the ruins as a child. Our school playing field at Cromford Meadows was opposite Cromford Mills and alongside Cromford Canal. It is widely acknowledged as one of the birth places of the Industrial Revolution, the source of the factory system and home to Sir Richard Arkwright. The mill complex built in 1771, a UNESCO World Heritage site, was the world's first successful water powered spinning mill.

There were numerous working textile mills in the Matlock area when I was growing up: Tor Hosiery producing stockings, Paton and Baldwin's woollen mill on Smedley Street, Drabbles bleach and dye works at Lumsdale, English Sewing Cotton at Masson Mill in Matlock Bath and John Smedley who still continue to manufacture since 1784 quality knitwear at Lea Mills.

The industrial history and architecture of my home town had always fascinated me and when I moved to Bradford on Avon it almost felt as though I was coming home.

Bradford on Avon

Bradford on Avon derives much of its character from its distinct topography: the river valley, the steep slopes rising from the valley floor and the numerous springs on the hillside. All of which, together with the wool, once considered the finest in the country, from sheep farmed in the region, the Cotswolds, the Marlborough Downs, Salisbury Plain, Wylye Valley and Cranborne Chase, contributed to its pre-eminence in the West Wiltshire woollen industry alongside nearby towns like Melksham, Trowbridge, Westbury, Warminster and surrounding villages. It was the high quality of its broadcloth for which Bradford on Avon became most famous and set it apart. Broadcloth was woven on extra wide looms to produce a dense, plain woollen cloth. This thick felted cloth was popular from the 15th to 17th century but as fashions changed in the 18th and 19th centuries, a superfine broadcloth became more popular.

The abundance of springs and underground water courses in the limestone delivered fresh water for wool washing to numerous stone tanks, troughs, cisterns, channels and ponds located at properties on the north side of the town. Many of these still exist as ornamental garden troughs and ponds. The Methuen family in the 17th century installed cisterns to hold the water in the Conduit House on Newtown, the site of the original medieval Lady Well, and connected it via a network of pipes and conduits to their workers' homes and workshops, including the Methuen family home at The Priory nearby. These provided an unfailing natural water supply. It has even been suggested that some of this lead pipework dates back to Roman times though there is no tangible proof to that effect. A local historian told me that there was evidence of lead pipework from the 18th century in a culvert of 17th century construction. I was shown fragments of lead pipework by the developers when the Victorian school buildings on Newtown were demolished and the land cleared for redevelopment.

Located immediately adjacent to the Conduit House, on the neighbouring site but at a significantly lower level underground, are more cisterns and the remains of a large circa mid 19th century iron water wheel measuring approximately 6 metres in diameter by 0.350 metres in width within a deep stone shaft. I did explore this dark underground site with some trepidation in the early 1980s. The wheel was relatively well preserved though in some state of decay, with water falling everywhere within the deep shaft. It is now, as then, largely inaccessible. A cloth factory previously existed on this part of the former 19th century Wilkins Brewery and Malthouse site. It is a matter for conjecture whether the water wheel was associated with the brewing and malting process, perhaps the most likely conclusion, or the woollen industry.

The proximity of the River Avon was central to the town's success. It provided water to the dye houses, such as the building which is now St Margaret's Hall, to the fulling mills and to power the industrialised workshops and to factories once the process became more highly mechanised. During the 18th and 19th centuries wool was washed in the river and strung across from one bank to the opposite side on timber frames. The remains of a wool washing island built from stone blocks is located in the river outside Abbey Mill.

The town was also well connected to transport routes since Roman times. Transportation improved at the beginning of the 19th century with the completion of The Kennet and Avon Canal in 1810, together with its connection to the short-lived Somerset Coal Canal at Limpley Stoke, and later Brunel's Great Western Railway opened in 1841. These carried goods in and out including coal from the Radstock Coal Field, used in later years to help power the mills and subsequently from 1834 to fuel Bradford's Gas Works. All these supply routes contributed to the success of the woollen industry.

Today the remains of the former cloth factories, the woollen mills with the weir upstream that served Kingston and Greenland Mills and the weir downstream at Avoncliff all contribute to the character of the town. The rich clothiers' houses, tightly packed rows of cloth workers cottages and steep hills, winding footpaths, narrow alleyways and steps, as well as the canal and railway create a distinctive pattern of development. They have resulted in Bradford on Avon becoming an attractive destination for tourism as well as a desirable place to live and work. This wasn't always the case!

The River Avon by Abbey Mill

Picture by Rosie MacGregor

Cloth Production and Mortality

There is archaeological evidence that as early as Roman times some cloth would have been woven in the area. Weaving of cloth commercially began in Bradford on Avon from the 12th to the 13th century as a predominantly cottage industry. However, it was not until the 15th century that the town's significance in the production of woollen cloth began to emerge with the manufacture of broadcloth, which was popular throughout Europe. The fashion for heavy broadcloth ceased by the middle of the 17th century and a finer quality cloth was in demand. There was need for change and improvement so Spanish wool began to be imported to enhance the quality of the product. In the mid-17th century Paul Methuen, one of the richest clothiers in the town, and

William Brewer a Trowbridge clothier, brought Flemish weavers from Amsterdam and Ghent to Bradford on Avon to help improve quality and to meet the demand of changing fashions. Methuen housed them at what is now known as Dutch Barton. These weavers not only introduced improvements to quality but new techniques. Inevitably there was resentment amongst local weavers.

The production of cloth was a highly labour intensive industry and most people living in the town, including children as young as seven, were employed in the various processes. Even those not directly employed in the industry were dependant on it for their own livelihoods.

The process of manufacturing woollen cloth for those working in the

Picture by Rosie MacGregor

Abbey House and Dutch Barton where Flemish weavers from Amsterdam and Ghent were housed. The gable end of Horton's House just visible at the rear of Abbey House

Picture: Trowbridge Museum Collection

A Patent Sheep Shearing Machine in action

industry in the 18th and 19th century Bradford on Avon involved not just skill but hard work and great care to produce a quality product. It would for the most part have been gruelling and repetitive work for which there was little recompense. The fleeces would originally have come from native breeds such as Cotswold and Lincoln, also known as Lindsey, sheep rather than the native Wiltshire Horn which had little wool and was bred for its meat. As early as the 13th century there are references to Lincoln sheep in Wiltshire. Later from the 18th century Merino sheep from Spain, but thought to have originated in North Africa, were bred in England for the improved quantity of fleece as well as the softness of the wool. There had been imports of Merino wool fleeces to England as far back as the 12th and 13th centuries but it was used for the production of poorer quality cloths rather than the heavy broadcloths produced in the West Country, which were exported to and favoured throughout Europe. Prior to the 18th century Spain held the monopoly on Merino wool and the export of live sheep was punishable by death! Indicative of the importance of wool for clothing.

Hand shears
Picture: Trowbridge Museum Collection

The wool fleeces first needed to be sorted and cleaned. The process required thorough cleansing known as scouring using water and stale urine to remove dirt, grease and any foreign particles such as burrs (seedpods) clinging to the fleece. The wool then needed to be scribbled on a frame in the weaving shed or workshop to remove any tangles ready for carding or combing using hand-held devices called carding hands. This ensured that there were no tangles and all the fibres were in long straight lines ready for spinning which twisted the wool into a tight yarn prior to weaving. Broadcloth manufactured in Bradford on Avon was a quality product woven on wide broadlooms requiring a minimum of two men to operate. Once woven the fabric then required fulling, also known as tucking, to cleanse,

Carding Hands
Picture: Trowbridge Museum Collection

bleach, soften and thicken the fabric by binding the threads close together and shrinking the cloth using a mix of Fullers' Earth, of which there was a plentiful supply locally, and once again stale human urine. This was collected daily by a cart collecting the urine from homes in the town and after three days the fresh urine would turn alkali which was essential to the process. Originally fulling was done by trampling the wool by foot in large tubs but by the 18th and 19th centuries this was carried out in purpose built water powered fulling mills where large wooden hammers called fulling stocks were used to strike and pound the cloth. Thereafter the cloth would be washed and if necessary dyed, during which process the urine was again used, this time as a mordant, a fixative to ensure the dye adhered to the cloth. The nap or pile would then be raised with teasels. Teasels can still be found today growing in cottage gardens throughout Bradford on Avon.

Picture by Rosie MacGregor

Teasels growing in gardens in Bradford on Avon — a reminder of the towns historic link to the woollen industry

Handle House in Stallard Street, Trowbridge next to the former Studley Mills

They would have been grown commercially in the past, soaked in water then dried in well ventilated buildings called 'handle houses', which had perforated brick walls to allow a free passage of air. None now remain in Bradford on Avon, all having been demolished. But one fine example remains in the centre of Trowbridge. The 19th century Handle House in Stallard Street, Trowbridge is Listed Grade II*. It is virtually unchanged since it was in use and is one of only a few such buildings that remain in this country and believed to be the only one in Wiltshire.

The teasels were fixed into wooden frames called handles which were drawn across the cloth to raise the nap by hand. The final process was shearing or cropping using large shears with a pair of 4-foot long blades to produce a good quality finish. This was the most skilled of all the processes which ensured that the cloth had a fine sheen and even finish. In order to produce the fine, close finish, for which Bradford on Avon was famed, the process would be repeated several times to raise the nap and shear the cloth.

Life for those working in the woollen industry was a constant struggle. They were desperately poor and their lifespan short. Apart from the wealthy clothiers, who traded in the woollen cloth, whose vast fortunes were made on the work of those they employed, wages were low and the work arduous with most families living hand-to-mouth. They had few material possessions and a severely restricted diet.

No wonder many workers resorted to the ale house, of which there were many, for comfort. They worked long hours and had no job security if they fell ill and were unable to work. Although advances were being made in medicine from the 17th century onwards, knowledge was limited and access to medical treatment was a dangerous luxury unavailable to the poor who relied on home remedies and

Picture: Bradford on Avon Museum Collection

The Three Horseshoes, known locally as 'The Shoes' one of the alehouses frequented by the cloth workers

improbable purges and potions as a curative for diseases and for the relief of pain. The link between poor hygiene and the spread of infection was not understood. Respiratory problems associated with the production of woollen cloth as well as diseases related to insanitary conditions and malnutrition as a result of poverty and poor diet were not uncommon. The Lady Well, a source of drinking water from mediaeval times, was frequently polluted. Life expectancy in the 18th and 19th century averaged no more than 40 years and even in death the working poor would have been buried in unmarked graves in which several bodies would have been interred. Infant mortality from diarrhoea, the exact causes uncertain, was high, particularly amongst the poor and rickets was a common ailment resulting from childhood malnourishment. There were regular outbreaks of cholera, typhus, typhoid, diphtheria, whooping cough and smallpox as well as consumption (tuberculosis) and other infections. All these as a result of deprivation and poverty associated with cramped and dirty living conditions, inadequate diet, poor sanitation, open sewers and contaminated water. The use of human urine in the process of washing, bleaching and fulling the wool was, somewhat surprisingly, not a health hazard!

Inequality and Impoverishment

Angry disputes between weavers and the other trades against the clothiers who employed them were not uncommon. Some employers accused their workforce of theft, which may not have been surprising given the low wages, and there was resentment too from those who were sacked or otherwise unemployed.

Most skilled workers from the 18th century onwards organised themselves in their different trades and all were threatened by the introduction of machinery.

There was a division of labour between the sexes in the different crafts. Historically most spinning was carried out by women and children. Prior to the production of broadcloth, weaving too was a job for women but due to the size of the looms and prior to mechanisation, broad loom weaving was a male preserve.

The large wooden looms necessary for weaving broadcloth were so wide that they required two weavers to carry out the process, one usually a master weaver and the other an apprentice learning the trade, passing the shuttle from one to the other.

Weaving was carried out initially in the weavers' homes and small workshops, at a later date within the mills. Once the weaving process became fully mechanised within factories it was women who operated the looms but customarily overseen by men.

The majority of fullers, dyers and shearmen, responsible for finishing the cloth, were male. Though there were some wealthy weavers who owned their own looms, the majority of hand-loom weavers lived impoverished lives alongside those working in other woollen trades, in overcrowded and neglected cottages and workplaces.

Weaver's cottages in Market Street, Bradford on Avon with larger upper windows

Though some weavers had hand looms within their homes, which can still be identified by larger windows on the top floor to gain maximum light, most were employed in small workshops necessary to accommodate several large looms required to weave the broadcloth and controlled by a master weaver.

Some of these workshops or weaving sheds were located adjacent to their houses. Their homes, often with just earth or flagstone floors and built into the limestone hillsides, were extremely damp and poorly maintained. Many of which, including those at Barton Orchard and Bearfield, were tenemented cottages occupied by several families living on different floors in squalid conditions for which they paid relatively high rents in comparison to the wages they received.

Picture: Bradford on Avon Museum Collection

Cloth workers houses in Newtown, Bradford on Avon

Despite Justices in Wiltshire attempting to set rates of pay for weavers, spinners, fullers and other cloth workers in the 17th century to alleviate their distress, it is doubtful if these were implemented by their employers. Given that these were maximum rates and differed for the various different cloth trades it is likely that there was no relief from destitution for most cloth workers, some of whom were paid in goods or tokens, known as truck, rather than money.

It was simply another way in which the workers were exploited by their employers. These tokens were a substitute for money, of lesser value and could only be exchanged locally, in certain shops and for services within the town over which the employers had a monopoly.

By the 18th century the cloth industry was central to the town's economy, indeed it was the principal industrial process in England at that time and something on which the clothiers relied for their wealth and on which their workers depended for the most basic standard of living.

Anxious clothiers throughout the West of England as early as 1718 and 1724 were complaining to Parliament of threats to burn property and destroy looms. By the mid 18th century the low rate paid for piece work was insufficient for weavers to earn even a basic living.

Faith and Deliverance

There is clear evidence that the clothiers exploited their workforce whilst growing rich on the profits. Compare their wealth and fine country estates and town houses to those of the labouring poor who were condemned to poverty and denounced for their alleged drunk and idle behaviour.

Thomas Horton a clothier in the late 15th and early 16th century who lived in a late mediaeval property now known as Horton House also owned Westwood and Iford Manors.

He built Holy Trinity Church Hall (now the Masonic Hall) and established the first school in the town in 1524 to educate boys, overseen by a priest employed by his own charity.

Thomas Horton's Charity was sadly short lived and was dissolved in 1540. He endowed The Chantry in Bradford on Avon with a priest to pray for his soul after his death. There is a brass memorial circa 1530 in Holy Trinity Church, the year of his death, to Thomas Horton and his wife who are both dressed in the finest clothes as you might expect of one of the wealthiest clothiers of the age.

The wealth of the earliest and most prosperous clothiers enabled them to be less dependent on the wool trade. They purchased land and great houses and diversified their investments.

The Hall, Grade I Listed and undoubtedly one of the finest buildings in the town, was rebuilt by the Hall family on the site of an earlier dwelling at the beginning of the 17th century.

This rich family of merchants and gentlemen once owned corn and grist mills as well as wool mills adjacent to the river run by clothiers.

Picture by Rosie MacGregor

The Hall, one of the finest Elizabethan houses in the area and home to the Hall family and later the Moulton family.

Picture by Rosie MacGregor

The Men's Almshouses in Frome Road, Bradford on Avon — and below the family coat of arms on the building

There is some dispute as to whether the Halls were clothiers themselves, and contradictions remain in the records.

However, in a town dominated by the wool trade it is more than likely that they were closely associated with the local industry. The Halls, together with the Horton and Rogers families, had dominated commerce and cloth making in the town from the 13th century.

John Hall built and endowed the Men's Almshouses on Frome Road in 1700. These buildings still bear the family coat of arms with the inscription "Deo et pauperibus", in other words "for God and the poor".

How successful this might have been in alleviating poverty or even ensuring John Hall's place in heaven is questionable as there were only four dwellings!

Picture by Rosie MacGregor

Corsham Court, the Methuen family home

It was, however, a charitable act though also I suggest a vanity project that has ensured his name is remembered more than 300 years later.

Belcombe Court, a fine Grade I Listed country mansion on the edge of the town, has earlier origins but it was rebuilt in 1734 by Francis Yerbury, one of the wealthiest clothiers.

It is indicative of his wealth that he was able to employ the visionary Architect John Wood the Elder who designed Prior Park, Queens Square and The Circus in Bath and was described by Nikolaus Pevsner as one of the most outstanding architects of the day.

The Hall family purchased Great Chalfield Manor. The Methuen family not only moved to Corsham Court which they extended and remodelled at great expense but enlisted the services of the famous landscape architect, Lancelot 'Capability' Brown known as 'England's greatest gardener' to landscape the park and garden. They also owned other property including a substantial house in London and amassed a vast and important collection of fine art. The Shrapnel family purchased Midway Manor and gave their name to the shrapnel shell invented by Major-General Henry Shrapnel an artillery officer in the British army.

These clothiers left a legacy of great houses, beautiful gardens and material possessions. Even in death the wealthy clothiers are commemorated by fine tombstones in local graveyards, and memorials from the 17th century onwards in Holy Trinity Church include those of Anthony Methuen and Francis Yerbury. Their lives and the luxuries they enjoyed, so different from the impoverished lives of those they employed.

Yet the cloth workers were an equally proud lot, proud of the work they did and proud of their non-conformist religion, despite a predilection for meeting in the numerous public houses in the town!

Picture by Rosie MacGregor

Memorial to clothier, Francis Yerbury in Holy Trinity Church, Bradford on Avon

Picture by Rosie MacGregor

Memorial to clothier Anthony Methuen in Holy Trinity Church, Bradford on Avon

The Congregational Church in St Margaret's Street, Bradford on Avon, now the United Methodist Church.

Non-conformist religion thrived in Bradford on Avon. The Society of Friends, or Quakers, were prominent in the town from the mid 17th century through until the mid 18th century. The Zion Baptist Chapel in Middle Rank was built in the late 17th century, the Baptist Chapel in St Margaret's Street was founded in 1689 but rebuilt in 1797, the Providence Baptist Chapel in Bearfield Buildings also dates from the late 17th century, the Congregational Church in St Margaret's Street was built in 1740,

The Countess of Huntingdon's Chapel in Huntingdon Street, Bradford on Avon dates from 1789 and is still used for evangelical worship today

and the Countess of Huntingdon's Chapel in Huntingdon Street dates from 1787. Perhaps because of the proximity of Bristol, there were frequent visits to the town by John and Charles Wesley who preached in open air meetings that attracted vast crowds. The largest of which was in 1739 when John Wesley preached to over 1,000 at Bearfield. This thriving Methodist community resulted in the building in 1756 of a Wesleyan Chapel in Market Street, at which John Wesley regularly preached, and is now a Snooker Hall forming part of the Town Club, and in 1818 of a second Wesleyan

Ruined Wesleyan Church in Coppice Hill, Bradford on Avon. The impressive external walls and front facade are all that remain of this Grade II* Listed Building built in 1818.

Church at the top of Coppice Hill, now a ruin and forming part of a private garden.

The names of the wealthy are remembered but the names of the ordinary people who worked in the woollen industry remain for the most part unrecorded and untraceable. Even in death they remained invisible with no headstone or memorial on a pauper's grave.

An Impossible Situation

The prosperity of the clothiers and their workers was interlinked. One so clearly dependent on the other so it is surprising that such scant regard was paid by employers to the wages and conditions of those they employed. The clothiers certainly cared about their own comfort and the quality of the cloth that their workers produced but they paid little attention to their workforce other than to castigate them when they took any action.

A group of shearmen had marched through Trowbridge in 1677 demanding improved pay but the first documented riot in Bradford on Avon did not take place until November 1726 in a dispute over increased work for reduced pay when there was also rioting in Trowbridge and Melksham. It is alleged that a great number of weavers stoned the houses and forced entry into the homes of several clothiers putting them in fear for their lives and making them promise to agree to their demands. Troops were called in and the High Sheriff read a proclamation (from the 1714 Riot Act) ordering the rioters to disperse. Refusal was a felony that could result in the death penalty but there was some sympathy for the rioters and they were treated with leniency. Though one rioter was killed, only one arrest was made and

Carding machine in Trowbridge Museum

Trowbridge Museum Collection by Roy McDine

he was subsequently pardoned. Perhaps even more surprisingly accounts of these riots were reported as far away as in the Ipswich Journal in Suffolk and Edinburgh's Caledonian Mercury. Francis Yerbury, the wealthy Bradford clothier, was summoned to quarter sessions on the information of a worker and found guilty of paying a fuller in goods rather than money.

Looms were broken in Melksham in the 1730s. An application to the magistrates in Melksham for poor relief was refused and troops were called to disperse rioters there. Conditions did not improve and in 1738 Henry Coulthurst, a wealthy clothier from Melksham, had his house and his chattels, his mills and nine cottages wrecked and woollen yarn thrown into the River Avon by angry weavers when he reduced payments to them. Three rioters were tried, found guilty and hanged but this did not prevent further riots in 1747 and 1750 when troops were again sent in to keep order.

The Industrial Revolution from the middle of the 18th century brought expansion of the industry and resulted in workers being employed in larger workshops and small factories where the threat of greater mechanisation caused further unrest. Before the mid 18th century the only widely used machines were the fulling stock, carding machine and gig mill, of which some were literally horse powered before the introduction of steam power. The Spinning Jenny, invented by James Hargreaves in 1764, was in use in parts of the west country towards the end of the century but they were not as widely used in West Wiltshire as elsewhere and not introduced into Bradford on Avon until around 1787. When the west country clothiers met in Bath in October 1776 it had been erroneously claimed that the Spinning Jenny would not lead to any unemployment, yet by the 1790s it had resulted in widespread job losses. There was greater acceptance of these machines by the end of the 18th Century within a booming cloth trade but not the shearing frame, invented by John Harmer of Sheffield in 1787, because the well organised, highly skilled and relatively well paid shearmen would have lost the most from its introduction.

There were at least two further major riots in Bradford on Avon in the 18th century, the first in 1787 over weavers' wages. It seems almost inconceivable that the clothiers promised not to erect further larger loom shops provided that the weavers would accept a reduction in rates of pay.

One particularly well documented violent act took place in 1791 in the town. Joseph Phelps, a wealthy clothier living at Westbury House in the centre of the town, fired on what was described as a mob of some 500 workers who rose up in anger. They were opposed to the introduction of a scribbling machine for carding the wool, which would have put many out of

Picture : Trowbridge Museum Collection

Spinning Jenny

work. Their demands were that he should hand over the machinery and continue to employ the hand scribblers. When he refused the workers and their families fearing destitution began to throw stones and allegedly damaged the building and broke some windows. There is little evidence of any major damage to this substantial house. Phelps and a friend initially brandished unloaded guns but when this had no effect they then fired loaded guns at the rioters killing three of them – a man, a woman and a child (Richard Naish, Elizabeth Tucker and James Bancroft), wounding two more, a man and a boy, who died later, and injuring others. Phelps and his men afterwards claimed they fired on the rioters in self-defence. Phelps subsequently handed over the machine to prevent further violence and it was burnt on Bradford on Avon Bridge by those who had taken part in the riot.

Picture: Bradford on Avon Museum Collection

Three Gables and Westbury House

The unarmed rioters could have been vindicated for defending their livelihoods and their way of life but the local establishment took a very different view. We must acknowledge that the employers saw mechanisation as the most profitable way forward but given the dependence of the clothiers' wealth on their workforce this episode is indicative of the scant regard they had for the conditions and livelihoods of those they employed. The firing on his workers and their families cannot reasonably be justified yet the coroner's verdict was to award Phelps £250 and record that it was 'justifiable homicide'. Those arrested for their part in the riot were shown some sympathy and later acquitted at the summer assizes. Troops were subsequently stationed in the town to prevent further rebellion. The majority of these were despatched in August 1792 to quell striking miners in the Mendip coalfield at Camerton though detachments were still stationed

in Bradford on Avon and surrounding villages until 1795. Following the Westbury House riot, Francis Hill, a Bradford clothier, moved his business to Malmesbury where the wool trade had previously ceased, taking with him some workers from Bradford on Avon, and set up a successful factory there in a former corn mill.

Scribbling Engines were first patented in a useable form by Richard Arkwright in 1775. It was claimed that one man and a boy using the machine could do the work of twenty scribblers. Hardly surprising then that there was prolonged resistance to their introduction leading to the riot at Westbury House. This invention proved central to the creation of an industry soon to be dominated by factories. Despite the riot Phelps did eventually manage to introduce machinery and the inventory following his death in 1794 included two scribbling engines and two carding machines.

The Shearmen

You have only to read Professor Adrian Randall's excellent book *Before the Luddites - Custom, Community and Machinery in the English Woollen Industry 1776–1809* to realise that resistance to the poor working conditions, deprivation and innovation in the woollen industry began long before the mass introduction of machinery and the Luddite insurgency of 1811–12. It was not so much resistance to the new ways of working but realisation of the negative impact that new machinery would have on their traditional crafts and the harm this would have on the communities in which the workers lived. Adrian Randall, Emeritus Professor of Birmingham University's History Department, who grew up in Bratton and attended school in Trowbridge, cites the story of Thomas Helliker as his own starting point for an outstanding career in history.

The industrial revolution brought greater mechanisation and workers feared the introduction of shearing frames to finish the cloth in local mills throughout West Wiltshire. It was alleged that groups of cloth workers, their faces blackened with soot to hide their identity, raided mills in a concerted attempt to destroy the hated machinery. The shearmen stood to lose the most from the introduction of machinery and were well-organised in both the North of England and the West Country in fighting this mechanisation. Shearmen, also known as cloth dressers, or croppers in Yorkshire, were amongst the most skilled and highly paid workers in

Picture from Trowbridge Museum Collection

Shears with four foot long blades used by shearmen to produce high sheen and an even, close finish on high quality broadcloth

the woollen industry. Their job was not to cut the cloth but to finish it by shearing it flat to produce a fine soft sheen after it had been washed and the nap raised by teasels. Shearmen from Bradford on Avon were amongst a group of Wiltshire workers intent on destroying mills in Twerton, Bath in 1798 where shearing frames had been installed and troops were again deployed.

The story of Helliker, sometimes known as The Trowbridge Martyr, is well known locally. Born in 1783 into a

Trowbridge family employed as cloth workers he was apprenticed as a shearman at the age of 14 and might in time have expected significantly higher earnings than weavers or other cloth workers. When shearing frames were introduced at Littleton Mill near Semington it was burned to the ground on 22 July 1802. Thomas was accused although he had an alibi, and protested his innocence. It is doubtful that Thomas took any part in the destruction of the mill. The mill was owned by Trowbridge clothier Francis Naish to whom Thomas was apprenticed and was managed by Ralph Heath who lived on the premises and had been forewarned of a likely attack by shearmen. Four or five men allegedly with blackened faces and armed with various weapons including pistols broke in at about one o'clock in the morning. Heath claimed to have recognised Thomas Helliker, even though it was dark, as one of the men who had stood guard over him whilst the other men set fire to the mill. Thomas was subsequently arrested and taken to Fisherton Goal in Salisbury. That evening Naish's workshops in Trowbridge were set alight in protest and burned to the ground. Numerous shearmen were arrested including John Helliker but only Thomas was charged and found guilty. Witnesses claimed that Thomas had been drunk that very evening and had been locked in a house for his own safety and would not have been able to undertake the journey to Littleton let alone stand guard over the mill manager.

Reports of the trial at the time described Thomas as a good looking youth. Afterwards at a later date, perhaps in an attempt to defame him, it was suggested that he had buck teeth and was a simpleton. The latter is highly unlikely given that he was an apprentice shearman, one of the most highly skilled trades in the wool industry. The jury took only 10 minutes to deliberate and declare him guilty. He languished in goal for a further week whilst his supporters fought frantically for a reprieve until the sentence was carried out. Even the press who had condemned the actions of the shearmen expressed sympathy for his case.

Thomas was hanged on his 19th birthday 22 March 1803 at Fisherton Gaol in Salisbury. It is generally accepted that he was innocent and in all probability was framed by powerful clothiers determined to make an example to prevent similar insurrection. Thomas may very well have known the culprits, and some suggest an older brother Joseph Helliker or even John Helliker may have been involved, but he refused to inform on them.

His body was removed from Salisbury and taken to St James Churchyard in Trowbridge by his supporters.

Reports tell of his remains being carried on a cart across Salisbury plain accompanied by a procession that grew larger as it reached his home town accompanied by girls dressed all in white forming a guard of honour.

The Rector had refused to bury the body in consecrated ground but was absent when Thomas's body was brought to the churchyard. John Rees, his young Welsh Curate, carried out the burial with full Christian rites after nightfall. It is alleged that John Rees, in order to gain an inheritance, changed his name to Rees-Mogg.

The finest carved chamber tombstone in St James Churchyard is that of Thomas Helliker. It was paid for by public subscription and erected by the shearmen of Yorkshire, Wiltshire and Somerset. The exact location of Thomas's grave within the churchyard is unknown as there have been many changes to the layout over the centuries and the tomb was in such poor repair in 1876 that it was removed for restoration. This fell into disrepair again and over the years his story became largely forgotten, except within the town itself. This tomb was restored by Trowbridge Trades Council in the 1980s and White Horse (Wiltshire) TUC hold a commemorative wreath laying there on 22 March of each year.

The original inscription on the tomb was dutifully contrite: "He died a true penitent being very anxious in his last moments that others might take a timely warning and avoid evil company" but when it was restored by clothworkers in 1876 the following words were added. "He was afterwards believed to be innocent but determined rather to die than give testimony which would have saved his life but forfeited the lives of others".

The original inscription on the tomb in full is as follows:

———◆◆———

Sacred to the memory of
Thomas Helliker
The thread of whose life was cut in the bloom of
youth
He exchanged mortality for immortality
March 22 1803
in the 19th year of his age.
The fatal catastrophe which led to this
unfortunate event is too awful to describe.
Suffice it say that he met his death with the

greatest fortitude and resignation of mind.
Considering his youth he may be said to have
but few equals. He died a true penitent. Being
very anxious in his last moments that others
might take a timely warning and avoid
evil company.
This tomb was erected at his earnest
request by the cloth making factories of the
counties of York Wilts and Somerset as a
token of their love to him and veneration of his
memory.

———◆◆———

The later inscription added (to the other side of the tomb) in 1876 reads as follows:

———◆◆———

This tomb was formerly placed over the remains
of
Thomas Helliker
At a time of great disturbance throughout the
manufacturing towns of this county. He was
condemned for an offence against the law of
which he was afterwards believed to be innocent
and determined to die rather than give testimony
which would have saved his own life, but
forfeited the lives of others.
Some of the cloth-workers of this town being so
desirous to perpetuate the remembrance of such
an heroic act of self-sacrifice have restored this
memorial in the year of our lord 1876.

———◆◆———

Helliker's tomb in St James' churchyard in Trowbridge

The Trowbridge and Bradford on Avon shearmen, after blackening the cloth and refusing to work, went on strike in 1802. John Jones, an eminent local builder, quarry owner, clothier and magistrate who lived in Bradford on Avon, had established a mill at Staverton in 1802 on the site of an earlier mill which he demolished. It was the largest water powered mill in the area on six storeys and with three water wheels. The Staverton Superfine Woollen Manufactory heralded the future for an industrialised woollen trade feared by a workforce who saw their traditional way of life and their livelihoods, however meagre these might have been, threatened. It was the scene of a number of riots in 1802.

John Jones, whose cloth had been woven and the nap raised ready for finishing on his gig mills in Staverton took the cloth to his finishing shops in Bradford on Avon for shearing. Jones had offered payment of 4 pence per yard, whereas the accustomed price was 7 pence per yard, for which he expected the men to work from six in the morning to six at night with only two breaks instead of the customary five. Jones reacted to intimidation by installing shearing frames in the mill at Staverton using non-shearmen to operate them. Despite negotiations between Jones and the Bradford on Avon shearmen, no solution to the dispute was found and the strike continued and prompted further attacks on his mill. The final one of which resulted in shots being fired between the attackers and Melksham Yeomanry. The attackers were not caught but the following night an empty dwelling house owned by Jones at Bearfield was burned

down. Jones was not alone in being attacked. Thomas Tugwell, another Bradford clothier, was a victim of the shearmen when his ricks were burned. A letter was found under the door of his workshops threatening his death and to cut out his heart for starving the poor. Tanner, another clothier from Bradford on Avon also had a large rick burned.

The introduction of machinery in Staverton resulted in a prolonged campaign of harassment against Jones who as a magistrate had endeavoured to suppress the riots of 1802. The workers endeavoured to establish a case in Parliament that the introduction of machinery was illegal but they lost. Perhaps not such a surprise given that Jones was chairman of the Bath committee supervising the clothiers case before parliament. Jones was subsequently shot and suffered a facial injury in 1808 as he rode home from Staverton to Bradford on Avon. A reward of £500 was offered to apprehend the culprits and three cloth workers from Bradford on Avon were arrested in 1812. One was never brought to trial, and without proof, the case against the remaining two was subsequently dismissed and they were acquitted. All was to no avail and by 1813 there were 40 looms in operation at Staverton Mill although the mill was no longer in Jones's ownership having been purchased by Thomas Joyce who owned factories in Bradford on Avon and Freshford. Jones had been made bankrupt in 1812, his finances having been severely over stretched in building Staverton Mill. He died a broken man soon after. It is said 'What goes around comes around' and it was Jones in his role as magistrate who had been instrumental in the arrest of Thomas Helliker.

There was further violence from angry shearmen in Bradford on Avon in 1807 and again in 1808 targeting the firm of Divett, Price and Jackson, wool merchants originally from Smithfield, London who had moved from London to Bradford on Avon in 1807 to establish their own finishing mills. Thomas Divett had first begun to move this operation to Bradford on Avon when he purchased The Hall, also known as Kingston House, in 1805. He replaced an existing mill to the south west of the dwelling with a purpose built cloth mill (Kingston Mill) and used the house for storage of wool, resulting in this fine building becoming neglected and falling into disrepair. Divett, Price and Jackson abandoned their manufacturing operation after less than ten years in 1816 and rented out their mill premises to other clothiers.

Troops had once again been deployed from 1807 until 1808 but failed to prevent a riot at the house of a John Adams.

Five shearmen were convicted at petty sessions for refusing to work with a man who had continued to work throughout the dispute but their sentences were quashed on appeal.

Ultimately the cloth workers, predominantly shearmen, were powerless against the might of the clothiers, mill owners, justices and troops. An upturn in the cloth trade combined with the need to modernise and increase production saw the end of any sustained violence or direct action for the time being.

Bradford on Avon Town Bridge with Kingston Mills on the right

Peace, Poverty and Propaganda

The end of the Napoleonic Wars (1803–1815) led to uncertainty in the woollen industry. Manufacturing of cloth for military uniforms at the start of the wars had resulted in a boom in trade but this did not last and afterwards exports of cloth declined.

The aftermath of the wars resulted in great misery and an increase in the population, higher taxes, rising food prices, poverty and unemployment placing great strain on poor relief.

Soldiers returning home after the Battle of Waterloo, where an estimated 17,000 had died, were for the most part in jubilant spirit only to find jobs were scarce and wages falling. There was considerable unrest and a sense of betrayal by the government amongst the working class. Public opinion was changing and Napoleon once regarded as the enemy was now seen by some, especially the poor, as a folk hero and the Establishment as their opponent!

Such sympathy for the 'bold Napoleon' together with a belief that the only ones to benefit from the wars were the British aristocracy became relatively commonplace. This is evidenced by the huge number of broadside ballads expressing sympathy or even praise for Napoleon published by a host of different printers at the time such as "Bonaparte's Farewell to Paris", "John Bull and Bonaparte", "Napoleon's Lament", "The Bonny Bunch of Roses O" and perhaps my favourite "The Grand Conversation on Napoleon Arose" published after Napoleon's death.

There was a distinct change in the tone of these ballads over time; at the start of the Napoleonic Wars when he was regarded as the enemy and after Waterloo when he is seen as a fallen hero. Prior to Waterloo the songs and broadsides caricatured Bonaparte and spread fear of imminent invasion calling for volunteers to fight the foreign foe. Few broadsides included music notation but popular tunes were sometimes suggested and were sung by the sellers to increase their circulation and were passed on by word of mouth and survived through the oral tradition. Many of these ballads had strong tunes which have endured until today having been collected by various collectors of folk song.

The introduction of the Corn Laws from 1815 exacerbated the wretched situation by imposing tariffs on the import of foreign grain resulting in greater food shortages, higher prices, increased hardship and a down turn in the economy. The inflated cost of wheat increased the price of bread, part of the staple diet of the labouring poor, and effectively resulted in little more than a starvation diet for many. Whilst the poor suffered, the wealthy country landowners grew rich on profits from the sale of grain. All this at the expense of the economy and manufacturing industries. The sale of manufactured goods fell as a greater proportion of everyone's income needed to be spent on food.

Hardly surprising then that there was discontent especially at a time when the cost of mechanisation of the woollen industry and a decline in trade was increasing the hardship for both worker and master. There were disturbances in Bradford on Avon in 1816 at the introduction of the flying-shuttle, invented by John Kaye in 1733 and in 1822 when spring looms were attacked following attempts to reduce weavers' wages. The decline in the cloth industry accompanied by a decline in wages resulted in further disturbances in 1816, again in 1819–20, 1826 and early in 1830 in the town. There were further strikes including from 1825 to 1829 when cloth workers across Wiltshire, Somerset and Gloucestershire took action. Though Bradford initially fared better than other wool towns in the area, by the 1820s work was short, wages reduced and several mills were forced to close as a result of bankruptcy. The workers feared for both their jobs and their way of life at a time when many found themselves jobless and destitute. For some there was no option but to take their own lives and four suicides were recorded in one day in 1821. William Cobbett in 1826 tells of factory workers from Bradford having no alternative but to walk miles to Heytesbury to gather nuts. An improbable distance of nearly 30 miles.

The purpose of propaganda is to disseminate information with the aim to persuade and influence public opinion often for a political cause. We should not assume that it is always a malign influence but necessary to build awareness of injustice. The producers of broadsheets or broadsides and pamphlet literature in the 19th century were well aware that these were powerful tools in promoting ideas, spreading knowledge, and winning hearts and minds. They were produced in large quantities and printed on one side of poor quality paper, making them cheap and easily accessible to a wide audience. Very often two ballads were printed lengthwise on the paper which could then be cut in half ensuring greater profit, or two for the price of one, and sold by itinerant sellers or balladeers. They would more often than not recite or preferably sing the ballad on street corners, at markets and fairs and in other public places. It made these ballads and songs immensely popular though the literary merits of some of them is not great.

Economic life after the Napoleonic Wars (1803-1815) and the Corn Laws (1815)

Export market for the cloth trade .... ↓
Jobs market .... ↓
Wages .... ↓
Food supply .... ↓
Sale of manufactured goods .... ↓
Country's economy .... ↓
Confidence in the Establishment .... ↓
Napoleon's image as a foreign enemy .. ↓
Population growth .... ↑
Unemployment .... ↑
Taxes .... ↑
Tariffs on imported grain .... ↑
Food prices .... ↑
Wealth of grain-growing landowners ..... ↑
Sense of government betrayal .... ↑
Poverty, destitution and suicides .... ↑
Belief that the war only benefitted the aristocracy .... ↑
Napoleon seen as a fallen hero .... ↑
General unrest .... ↑

It is surely no coincidence, given the dates which correspond with the discontent and upheaval in West Wiltshire from 1815 until the 1830s, that many broadsides in support of Napoleon and praising his bravery and heroic deeds survive from the same period. It would certainly be no surprise, given the impoverished state of the working class. The one printed here was published following Napoleon's death in May 1821 by James Catnach, a popular printer based at 2 & 3 Monmouth Court, Seven Dials, London who produced chapbooks, ballads and broadsides from 1813 until his death in 1842. There were other broadsides of the same title and with similar wording produced by different printers across the country that have also survived.

The Grand Conversation on Napoleon

It was over that wild beaten track a friend of bold Bonaparte
Did pace the sands and lofty rocks of St Helena's shore,
The wind it blew a hurricane, the lightning flash around did dart,
The seagulls were shrieking and the waves around did roar.
Ah hush rude winds the stranger cried, awhile I range the dreary spot
Where last a gallant hero his envied eyes close.
But whilst his valued limbs do rot, his name will never be forgot.
        This grand conversation on Napoleon arose.

Ah England why he cried did you persecute that hero bold?
Much better had you slain him on the plains of Waterloo.
Napoleon he was a friend to heroes all, both young and old,
He caused the money for to fly wherever he did go.
When plans were ranging night and day, the bold commander to betray,
He cried, I'll go to Moscow and there 'twill ease my woes.
If fortune smiles on me that day, then all the world shall me obey,
        This grand conversation on Napoleon arose.

Thousands of men he did then rise to conquer Moscow by surprise,
He led his troops across the Alps oppress'd by frost and snow,
But being near the Russian land, he then began to open his eyes,
For Moscow was a-burning, and the men drove to and fro;
Napoleon dauntless viewed the flame and wept in anguish for the same,
He cried, retreat my gallant men, for time so swiftly goes.
What thousands died on that retreat, some forced their horses for to eat.
        This grand conversation on Napoleon arose.

At Waterloo his men they fought, commanded by great Bonaparte,
Attended by Field Marshall Ney and he was bribed by gold.
When Blucher led the Russians to, it nearly broke Napoleon's heart.
He cried, my thirty thousand men are killed, and I am sold.
He viewed the plain and cried it's lost, he then his favourite charger crossed,
The plain was in confusion with blood and dying woes. The bunch of roses did
advance and boldly entered into France.
        This grand conversation on Napoleon arose.

Then Bonaparte was planned to be a prisoner across the sea,
The rocks of St Helena, it was the fatal spot.
Doomed as a prisoner there to be till death did end his misery.
His son soon followed to the tomb, it was an awful plot.
And long enough have they been dead, the blast of war is around spread,
And may our shipping float again to face the daring foes.
And now my boys when honour calls we'll boldly mount those wooden walls.
        This grand conversation on Napoleon arose.

Another broadside ballad that survives from 1829 is 'The Weavers' Turn-out' the meaning of which, to turn out, was that they were taking strike action. This street ballad was produced by Bonner & Henson, printers of 3 Narrow Wine Street, Bristol who produced a number of pamphlets between 1825 and 1830. Though this broadside probably originated as a result of industrial action being taken in Gloucestershire it refers to Bradford and Trowbridge. No tune, even if one ever existed, survives. Since the words don't scan easily and there is no trace of the song in the oral tradition it is unlikely that it was ever sung. However, these pamphlets or 'penny broadsides' as they were known were a successful form of propaganda. Used in this instance to publicise and inform the workers that they were not alone in seeking improvements to pay and conditions and to encourage them to take action. Trades unions began to emerge in the 18th century, though not strictly legal until much later, and the clubs referred to in the ballad were the mutual societies set up by groups of different craft workers which collected money from their membership and held funds to support those members and their families in need. Though not particularly well written, with numerous spelling errors (reproduced as published), the words clearly combine some sincere hopes with a trace of sarcasm towards the employers and a rousing chorus.

The Weavers' Turn-out

O, hark! my lads, and give an ear, to listen unto me,
A story unto you I'll relate which happen'd the other day,
It's concerning of weavers who for their rights maintain,
We have been labouring many a year, but still it was all in vain.

Chorus
So let us all, while in our bloom,
Drink success to the weavers' loom.

In Dursley town in Gloucestershire, for wages we stood out,
It was for one 3-pence per yard on a chain of broadcloth,
Our clubs we have to support our wives and children dear,
We live in hopes of better times while we drink a jug of beer.

Look all around the neighbourhood and you will quickly hear,
We are in hopes our employers our wages will ensure,
For provisions they are plentiful, they are so rich and good,
And so my boys we'll never fear our clubs they will stand good.

Behold the town of Bratford and Wotton under Hedge too,
The weavers they are all combin'd to their colors will stand true,
The town of Trowbridge as you hear and not leave Milsom out,
And all round the neighbourhood for wages will stand out.

All around the neighbourhood the trade it has been good,
For all mechanics in the trade to support themselves with food,
But the weavers they are valiant men as you will understand,
Then for our wages we stand out and no more be at command.

So to conclude my ditty and to finish up my song,
We'll drink success to the weavers, may the trade be carried on.
Likewise to our employers wherever they may they dwell,
May the trade be in a flourishing state, and never for to fail.

Numerous broadside ballads exist about weaving but none so poignant as those produced after the Napoleonic Wars and in the early part of the 19th century referring to the down turn in trade. Their titles only too clearly mirror the depressed state of the woollen industry and the distress of those affected including "The Weaver's Farewell to his Loom!", "I am a Poor Weaver and Forced to Roam" and "The Weaver's Lamentation".

A verse from one broadside published in the mid-19th century sums it up quite simply:

The children round about us cry
For bread but we can't supply
Their wants and every other aid,
For we have neither work nor trade.

A song specific to shearmen is "The Cropper Lads" although it originated later than the events in Wiltshire. It relates to machine breaking in West Yorkshire in 1812 by a group of some 100 Luddites, armed with hammers, hatchets and pistols, intent on destroying shearing frames at Rawfold's Mill near Huddersfield. They marched on the mill but William Cartwright, the owner, had been forewarned and was inside with soldiers awaiting the attack. A fierce fight ensued and many were injured including two of the ringleaders who were shot and afterwards died. Others were apprehended and several were subsequently hanged but like Helliker they refused to name anyone else involved in the attack. The Luddites were a group of radical textile workers who, fearing that the introduction of

machinery would destroy their livelihood, had sworn a secret oath to destroy the hated machinery. This provocative song is clearly not simply intended to commemorate the event but as a rallying cry to others. Great Enoch was apparently the name given to the heavy sledge hammers used to destroy the shearing frames. Ironically both the hammers and the shearing frames were manufactured by brothers Enoch and James Taylor, blacksmiths from Marsden, who claimed their shearing frames could do the work of ten men.

The Cropper Lads

Come Cropper lads of high renown
Who love to drink good ale that's brown
And strike each haughty tyrant down
With hatchet, pike and gun

Chorus:

Oh the Cropper lads for me
The gallant lads for me
Who with lusty stroke the shear frames broke
The Cropper lads for me

What, though the Specials still advance
And soldiers lightly round us prance
The Cropper lads still lead the dance
With hatchet, pike and gun

And night by night when all is still
And the moon is hid behind the hill
We forward march to do our will
With hatchet, pike and gun

Great Enoch still shall lead the van
Stop him who dares, stop him who can
Press forward every gallant man
With hatchet, pike and gun

Decline

Though early clothiers flourished and made huge profits this was not the case in later years. It would appear that there had been greater resistance to the introduction of machinery in the west country in comparison to Yorkshire. By the mid 19th century Bradford in West Yorkshire was known as the "wool capital of the world" with more than 300 textile mills in operation and Bradford on Avon and the woollen towns of West Wiltshire, Somerset and Gloucestershire were in decline. One reason undoubtedly was the reluctance to invest in machinery whereas Yorkshire had embraced the use of steam power and built vast mechanised factories, the number and scale of which dwarfed those in West Wiltshire.

Chartism (1838–1857) which called for the vote for all men over 21 and secret ballots amongst a raft of six demands proved popular in Bradford on Avon with down-trodden workers in the woollen industry hoping that parliamentary reform would result in a rise in their fortunes and greater prosperity in the industry. In September 1838 a group of 15,000 Chartists converged on Trowle Common between Bradford on Avon and Trowbridge at a mass meeting addressed by Henry Vincent, a charismatic orator and Chartist leader from London who was at that time based in Bath, and local Chartist firebrand and cloth worker William Carrier from Trowbridge. It proved a momentous success combining passionate speeches and a call to arms much to the alarm of the local magistrates, mill owners and gentry. Torchlight processions and rallies in neighbouring towns were to follow but after the arrest of local ringleaders from Trowbridge and Westbury and their subsequent imprisonment the early enthusiasm disintegrated.

In Bradford on Avon in 1841, the year the census was carried out, "the once-prosperous cloth industry was brought to a standstill, when the chief local Bank featured in the bankruptcy court; and when the workhouse at Avoncliff was strained beyond capacity by a sudden influx of unemployed and their dependants", quote from *Year of the Map*.

Picture: Bradford on Avon Museum Collection

The Bradford Union Workhouse at Avoncliff. Built to house cloth workers it became a workhouse, then hospital and it's now houses

Picture by Rosie MacGregor

The Hobhouse, Phillott & Lowder Bank in Church Street, Bradford on Avon. Now a private house and Listed Grade II*

The failure of the Hobhouse, Phillott & Lowder Bank with its prestigious offices in Church Street, Bradford on Avon and Milsom Street, Bath was caused by the bank over stretching its lending commitments for many years and this had far reaching implications with clothiers made bankrupt and many workers left destitute. There was widespread unemployment, those who retained their jobs found their wages reduced whilst the price of food and other essentials were again on the increase.

Those admitted to the workhouse, which was overwhelmed, had for the most part been skilled in different trades within the cloth making industry. Many of those who continued to live in their own homes were recipients of charity or poor relief, and some were driven to suicide.

There was widespread despair and poverty and many of the cloth workers were forced to emigrate, often to work in the textile mills of the United States where conditions were little better than at home.

There were 21 firms making cloth in Bradford on Avon at the beginning of the 19th century but by 1841 this had reduced to no more than four employing around 400 people. This was the start of a period in our history known as the Hungry Forties when the whole country fell into deep economic recession.

This depression combined with the failure of the potato crop which ravaged Europe, albeit far worse in Ireland and Scotland, resulted in widespread misery, hunger and starvation.

Following the failure of the principal bank some clothiers were made bankrupt. The lack of foresight either as bankers in lending money or as men of property and influence is astonishing as they clearly misjudged the situation.

Many clothiers had been reliant on unsecured bank loans which they had been unable to repay. When the bank failed as a result of over lending, economic fluctuations in the woollen trade and default on repayments, they lost everything. There was also the failure of the manufacturers to invest when they needed to modernise.

The distress of the cloth workers in Bradford on Avon following the rapid decline in the industry was reported in The Sun newspaper on 10 January 1842 after a meeting of woollen manufacturers from Gloucester, Wiltshire and Somerset in Bath.

There had been 19 manufacturers in Bradford on Avon producing 620 pieces of broadcloth each week in 1820 and it was reported that the town was relatively prosperous whereas in 1842 there were only two manufacturers and production had reduced to 100 pieces of cloth per week.

There were at that time 462 looms in the town of which 316 were lying idle,

135 partly so and only 11 working at full capacity. This left an estimated 1082 individuals, more than one quarter of the population (recorded as 3,836 in the census of 1841), without the means of employment and relying on parish relief.

There was widespread fear of the workhouse amongst the poor who dreaded the separation of husbands, wives and children, coupled with a routine of forced labour and denial. The indignity of what was akin to imprisonment, even though admission to the workhouse was supposedly 'voluntary' created a lasting stigma.

Yet there was no alternative for many. Despite the monotonous work and harsh regime at least the inmates were fed and clothed with a roof over their heads and their children would have received some basic schooling. Whilst we might assume that only a meagre diet was provided in the

Picture by Rosie MacGregor

Abbey Mill in Church Street, Bradford on Avon. The last woollen mill to be built in the town in 1875 and Listed Grade II*

workhouse this is far from the truth even in this time of great hardship. The allowance of bread and meat for inmates of the Bradford Union Workhouse at Avoncliff, originally built to house cloth workers in 1792 and converted into a workhouse in 1836 to accommodate 250 paupers, was significantly greater than the average diet of the labouring poor in the town. The unemployed were forced to undertake various public works which included making a new road from Belcombe to Turleigh and improving the gradient of the hill on the road to Trowbridge. Despite a massive influx of newcomers to the town from the late 20th century onwards, it can be seen from local surnames that the descendants of those whose names were recorded as inmates of the workhouse are still found living in Bradford on Avon and surrounding area, as are the names of the clothiers, their masters.

There was a brief revival of the wool trade from 1843 until the end of the century but wages remained low.

Hardly surprising that in 1845 between 50 and 60 cloth workers who worked from 6am to 7pm, except on Saturdays when they could leave at 3pm went on strike. Not for higher wages but because this was piece work and more than 3 extra yards of cloth was being added to their work for which their employers were refusing to pay.

Four strikers John Bell, Job Bell, John Angell and Daniel White were brought before Bradford Petty Sessions in April of that year by Messrs Edmonds, Clothiers. They were found guilty and fined 20 shillings each.

Abbey Mill, Listed Grade II*, is an imposing Gothic style building on 5 storeys dating from 1875 in Church Street. It was the last wool mill to be built combining both water power and steam with two tall chimneys, both since demolished. Production of cloth ceased in 1902.

Greenland Upper Mill which closed in 1906 was the last factory to manufacture woollen cloth.

Picture: Bradford on Avon Museum Collection

Greenland Upper Mill. Little remains of these buildings following a major fire at the five-storey building. The site was redeveloped for housing.

Good Clothiers

With the possible exception of 17 decent dwellings built on three sides of a square in 1792 by wealthy clothier John Moggridge to house his workers at Avoncliff and subsequently sold and converted into the Bradford Union Workhouse in 1836, there is no evidence of the type of philanthropy found elsewhere in the country. Notably the model established in 1776 by Sir Richard Arkwright at Cromford who built houses, a church, chapels, schools, shops and even a public house for his workers.

This model was followed by factory reformer Robert Owen at New Lanark in Scotland in 1799. His enlightened beliefs led to the creation of an industrial settlement beside the River Clyde where the welfare of his workers both spiritually and physically was paramount but equally ensured their productivity, commitment and loyalty.

The pattern was copied elsewhere, perhaps best represented by Victorian philanthropist Sir Titus Salt's Saltaire near Bradford, Yorkshire built between 1851 and 1876 where an entire village and woollen mill of exemplary classical style were built beside the River Aire.

Retired workers at Saltaire were even given a pension, as I discovered during a student visit on a week-long second year 'Field Trip' to Yorkshire.

No similar social conscience appears to have been displayed by the 'good' clothiers of Bradford on Avon. The Moggridge family were in partnership with other well-off clothiers in the town and neighbouring villages including the Yerbury and Joyce families.

Together they could have done much to alleviate the suffering of their workers but there is no other evidence apart from the 17 houses at Avoncliff of any benevolence towards their workers.

Picture: Bradford on Avon Museum Collection

The dark, cramped and overcrowded cottages in Hangdog Lane, Bradford on Avon that have since been demolished

Revival of Fortune

The story of Bradford on Avon might have been very different had it not been for Stephen Moulton returning from a visit to the USA in the middle of the 19th century with the knowledge of how to vulcanise rubber.

He established his own factory in the town in 1848 having purchased The Hall and Kingston Mills which gradually helped revive the town's economy. The vacant woollen trade buildings proved ideal to house this expanding new industry.

It was a defining moment for the town, which for the next 150 years became reliant on rubber processing. The last remaining examples of industry in the town today are the world famous Moulton bicycle and Anthony Best Dynamics, a company producing advanced vehicle testing systems.

The majority of original woollen mills, workshops and surrounding land have been now converted into residential use.

Buildings and their uses change over time and alterations are made which involve the loss of important historic characteristics such as the remnants of features necessary to their former use. The handle house that previously formed part of the Abbey Mill complex was demolished long ago to form the new heavy goods vehicle access into Abbey Mill after it became part of Avon Rubber.

Bradford on Avon underwent some slum clearances in the 1960s but suffered far less than Trowbridge where many historic buildings were demolished much earlier from the 1930s until the late 1960s.

The former workers' cottages on the steep hillside above the town were in a very poor state of repair by the mid 20th century and largely occupied by those living in poverty.

Bradford on Avon Urban District Council in the late 1950s proposed their demolition. Like so many English towns and cities Newtown, Tory, Middle Rank and parts of Wine Street and St Margaret's Hill area were to be compulsorily purchased as part of a

Bradford on Avon Museum Collection

The parade in 1910 commemorating the death of King Edward VII passes Church Street Mill with its the teasel drying floor. The perforations visible at high level in the external wall allowed circulation of air around the suspended handles of teasels as they dried.

Picture by Pete MacGregor

Church Street now, with the building that housed the teasel drying floor demolished to form the entrance to the rubber factory

slum clearance programme and replaced with council owned flats.

A campaign to save these properties started in Bradford on Avon in 1963 and gained national momentum resulting in the majority being saved and refurbished.

Unfortunately, some of the houses at the top of Wine Street and in St Margaret's Hill were subsequently demolished to make way for new council and speculative development at Budbury and council flats for the elderly at St Margaret's Hill.

But overall, Bradford on Avon had been lucky because its Preservation Trust, formed in 1964, fought successfully to prevent wholesale destruction. The social impact on the town has been relatively positive as a result with new uses found for the historic buildings including housing, retail and commercial.

Trowbridge townscape however was fundamentally changed in the 20th century, particularly in the Conigre area where Thomas Helliker had once lived, Yerbury Street and town centre.

All to make way for a bus station at the Conigre, vacant sites and swathes of car parking. The bus station has since been replaced and much needed new housing has been built but we should question whether this has been at the expense of the historic environment.

Some of the finest large industrial buildings that remain today, such as Innox Mill, have since fallen into disrepair without viable future new uses being found.

Even its unique Handle House had remained empty for more than a century without any alternative use found until it was refurbished and successfully converted into an office though this at the time of writing is currently unused.

Picture: Trowbridge Museum Collection

Workshops used for spinning and carding in Yerbury Street, Trowbridge which were demolished in the 1960s

Distaff Power and Control

If the male cloth workers had a hard time you can be assured that for women it was worse. Something that struck me when reading and researching the woollen industry in the area, as with most locations, is that the names of ordinary women are rarely if ever recorded except in the official lists of their births, deaths and marriages or their entry to the workhouse.

The lives of women are seldom mentioned in any other context. Yet they numbered the majority of spinners and many, once the process was mechanised, were weavers. They were wives and mothers and represented half the population. This was a male dominated society and women are all too often overlooked by history.

We know that women and children were present at the riots, the name of Elizabeth Tucker is recorded as having been killed at Westbury House, yet we know very little of their lives other than the work they did which was regarded as inferior to that of many of the male occupations.

Why for example was shearing the cloth, an entirely male preserve, regarded so highly compared with spinning and weaving, surely with a similar need for precision. It was men, obviously, who controlled the workshops but equally they controlled women's lives. Indicative of a patriarchal society and an industry dominated by men and one in which the wealthier the man, the greater his power.

These hard-working women not only spun and often wove the cloth, but cleaned the house, cooked the food, gave birth, looked after and educated their children, washed the linen, made and repaired the clothes, cared for the sick and elderly and supported their husbands and fathers.

Women's achievements throughout the past, with a few notable exceptions, have either been written out of history, forgotten and demeaned or given belated recognition long after their deaths.

It is the same narrative for women of the working class who almost always remain anonymous. Women have to work twice as hard as their male colleagues to get the recognition they deserve.

Whilst the wives of the wealthy clothiers in Bradford on Avon may have had limited rights they were at least cushioned from the hardships of daily life and enjoyed the privilege of fine clothes, good food and leisure, the women workers were subjected to privation and monotonous routine. Despite producing the finest cloth their own clothes were of the poorest quality.

The lives of women cloth workers were constrained by poverty and there was little escape from male control, caring for the family and the drudgery of workshop or factory.

A verse from a song in the ballad opera "The Country Bumpkin" written by Henry Cary in 1730 accurately reflects the position of women not just at the time he wrote it but through the centuries.

"Oh, hard is the fortune of all woman kind; She's always controlled, she's always confined; Controlled by her

Weaving Machines at Greenland Mills, Bradford on Avon

parents until she's a wife; A slave to her husband the rest of her life."

Marital conflict and assault, both physically and verbally of wives by their husbands, even though largely undocumented, would almost certainly have been prevalent amongst all classes of society and especially the working poor in the town as it was elsewhere in the country.

This would have been exacerbated by poverty, cramped living conditions and drunkenness. A favourite pastime being the ale house and accessibility of cheap liquor given the large number of public houses.

Moreover, the abuse of women in varying degrees by husbands who believed it was their absolute right was endemic in the 17th, 18th and early 19th centuries.

Women were regarded as little more than a chattel with few legal rights to property or money until the Married Women's Property Act of 1870. It was

culturally acceptable and legally sanctioned that husbands had the right to beat their wives as a form of correction.

The perpetrators were rarely reported partly because their wives, who usually suffered in silence, were fearful that if they complained their situation would only be made worse. Especially so if the husband was brought before the justices and fined or imprisoned.

This would only increase the financial hardship of the household. There was no escape from the marital home for most women and divorce was not an option for the poor even after the first divorce law The Matrimonial Causes Act of 1857.

Life was no better for the workers' children who were forced to work as soon as they were able, frequently as young as seven and often in dangerous working conditions. When children made mistakes their treatment was harsh and physical punishment the norm.

Conclusion

Bradford on Avon for the majority of those living here today is a lovely place to live but we must never forget the past. I well remember many years ago when I first moved to the town, living in a cottage on the top of the hill, where on warm summer nights with the bedroom windows open you could hear the reassuring hum of the night shift at Kingston Mills.

It was an industrial town then but no longer. Now more of a tourist destination and a dormitory town for nearby larger towns and cities but it still retains its community spirit and strong sense of place.

One final thought in what we might hope is a more enlightened age. There is an inexplicable but popular romantic notion that the occupation of weaver is somehow enviable and bestows some cachet to the value of the properties they once occupied.

The so-called Weavers Cottages, complete with fanciful names and roses round the door, previously occupied not just by weavers but cloth workers and artisans of every kind, are now desirable places to live.

Local residents might do well to remember the history of their well maintained, warm, dry and sophisticated homes that sell at a premium and spare a thought for the lives of those who went before.

Acknowledgements and thanks

Before the Luddites ....Adrian Randall
The Shearmen and the Wiltshire Outrages of 1802:
Trade Unionism and Industrial Violence ....Adrian Randall
Scabs and Traitors – Taboo, violence and punishment in
labour disputes in Britain 1760–1871..Thomas Linehan
West Country Rebels ....Nigel Costley
The Year of the Map. Portrait of a Wiltshire Town in 1841 ....Gee Langdon
Wool and Water ....Kenneth G Ponting
Warp and Weft..Kenneth H Rogers
The Domestic Woollen Industry at Bradford on Avon ....Kenneth H Rogers
The Machine Breakers ....Eric Hobsbawn
Protest, Politics and Work in Rural England, 1700–1850 ....Carl J Griffin
Textile History and Economic History Essays in honour of
Miss Julia de Lacy Mann ....edited by NB Harte and KG Ponting
The Violent Abuse of Women in 17th and
18th Century Britain ....Geoffrey Pimm
Marital Violence: An English Family History, 1660–1857................................Elizabeth Foyster
Bradford on Avon – a History and Description ....Canon Jones
The Buildings of England – ....Nikolaus Pevsner

Cobbett's Annual Register
British History on-line
The British Newspaper Archive
Bodleian Libraries Broadside Ballads on-line
Vaughan Williams Memorial Library
Wiltshire and Swindon History Centre
Bradford on Avon Museum

Thanks to Trowbridge Museum for the use of photographs of
historic wool processing machinery.
A very rare Spinning Jenny on loan from the
Science Museum, London can be seen on display in Trowbridge Museum.

Special thanks for help and advice to:
Nikki Ritson, Collections and Exhibitions Officer.
David Birks, Learning and Outreach Officer.
Contact: nikki.ritson@trowbridge.gov.uk Tel: 01225 751339

Bradford on Avon Museum deserves a special thanks for allowing use of old photographs of
the town. Special thanks also to
Ivor Slocombe, Local Historian, Pam Slocombe, Buildings Historian
Mervyn Harris, Honorary Chairman, Bradford on Avon Museum
Roger Clark, Honorary Curator, Bradford on Avon Museum for their help and advice

Myth busting

Despite a commonly held misconception Bradford, West Yorkshire did not gain its name from Bradford on Avon in Wiltshire.

Both towns derive their name from broad fords over rivers, and Bradford, Yorkshire and Bradford (on Avon) were both identified as such in Domesday of 1086.

However, the suffix 'on Avon' was added to Bradford in the late 19th century as its pre-eminence in the wool trade gave way to that other Bradford in West Yorkshire in order to avoid confusion between the two.

Until then if the town of Bradford was mentioned in the context of wool everyone knew it was our town, the name by which it had been known since the late Anglo-Saxon period!

Other books by Rosie MacGregor

Angela Remembered
The life of Angela Gradwell Tuckett
by Rosie MacGregor

ISBN 978-0-9570726-3-3
Published 2015

Angela Remembered is a celebration of the life of a feminist, peace campaigner, trade unionist, qualified air pilot, first woman solicitor in Bristol, journalist, folk musician and writer of songs, plays, poetry and books.

She joined the Communist Party after seeing the plight of hunger marchers in 1931 and in 1935 she caused a diplomatic incident when as a member of the England hockey team in Germany she refused to give the Nazi salute. At great personal risk she smuggled 'Red Aid' to the Greek Patriots in 1937.

She was Head of the Legal Department of the National Council for Civil Liberties in 1940 — then moved to The Daily Worker (now The Morning Star) as legal advisor and journalist before moving to Labour Monthly.

WILD WEST WILTSHIRE
Outlaws and Schemers

Fury as council chief is banned from office

Shock as council chief is suspended

Angry workers stage walk-out WHY ALL THESE SECRETS?
Reinstatement for suspended council chief
Two council officers 'paid more than Thatcher'
How town hall tycoons blundered, by civic watchdog

New probe rocks council as ex-Tories attack £8m deal

The West Wiltshire Council IT scandal
A personal reminiscence by Rosie MacGregor

ISBN 978-0-9957917-2-5
Published 2022

The improbable title of *Wild West Wiltshire — Outlaws and Schemers* may seem far-fetched but this book accurately describes scandalous events that took place in the late 1980s and early 1990s.

This is the unlikely story of goings-on in a quiet rural local authority in Wiltshire that brought the council into disrepute and had a lasting impact on those involved. It made national headlines at the time yet today the story is almost forgotten.

This book is a first-hand memory by a participant in the drama as it unfolded.

Rosie MacGregor tells the story from her own recollection, the memories of those involved and from press reports at the time.

Available from www.watermarx.co.uk